# THE NINE OF DIAMONDS

'Luscious, generous and always terrifyingly wise, MacGillivray's unique poetic intelligence has crafted a work we have all been secretly waiting for. Its voice and the crystal breath between the words awakens histories and futures that are vividly permeable to our memory and longing. A twilight cartomancy born between open heath and midnight cave; sublime in rage, quick in beauty and hopelessly decade to love.' – B. CATLING

*The Nine of Diamonds* is MacGillivray's second book of poetry. Her first, *The Last Wolf of Scotland*, was published by Pighog in 2013:

'There are not many books of poetry that can be classified as genuinely original and large in scope; even among the disputed ground of "innovative writing" there is little that is truly groundbreaking. Reading *The Last Wolf of Scotland*, however, I feel that I may have found just that sort of book.' – STEVEN WALING, *Magma*

# MacGillivray

# The Nine of Diamonds

## SURROIAL MORDANTLESS

BLOODAXE BOOKS

ISBN: 978 1 78037 324 9

First published 2016 by
Bloodaxe Books Ltd
Eastburn
South Park
Hexham
Northumberland NE46 1BS


www.bloodaxebooks.com
For further information about Bloodaxe titles
please visit our website or write to
the above address for a catalogue.

Supported using public funding by
ARTS COUNCIL
ENGLAND

Cover design: Neil Astley & Pamela Robertson-Pearce.


Printed in Great Britain by Bell & Bain Limited, Glasgow, Scotland, on
acid-free paper sourced from mills with FSC chain of custody certification.

# 9 ♦

'shaping sand from thistle covered fog'
PHILIP LAMANTIA, 'The Islands of Africa'


'stags with antlers of coral'
ANDRÉ BRETON, 'Freedom of Love'


'there was a still pool in the garden's eye'
DAVID GASCOYNE, 'Future Reference'


'so this rainbow look'd like hope
Quite a celestial kaleidoscope'
LORD BYRON, *Don Juan:* Canto the Second

'If a person happens to be deprived of his senses, the deranged cells of the brain must be adjusted by the magic charms of the anti-conjurer...'

JOHN BRAND, *Observations of Popular Antiquities*, III (1842)


In that case, for Clan Quhettane Sossery.

# STAKES

'JUNE 26 1786. Mr Urban, a Correfpondent in your March magazine expressing a defire to know the origin of the nine of diamonds being called "the Curfe of Scotland", I beg leave to offer the following explanation, which, I have been affured, is the true: That the night before the battle of Culloden, the Duke of Cumberland thought proper to fend orders to General (Campbell, I think, but am not quite certain) not to give quarter; and, this order being difpatched in much hafte, happened to be written on a card, and that card was the nine of diamonds; from which time and circumftance it has gone by the appellation in queftion.'

# PACE 1

## SUIT OF
## THE GAELIC GARDEN
## OF THE DEAD

THE DIVINATION BY the taghairm was once a noted super-stition among the Gaels of Scotland. When any important question concerning futurity arose and of which a solution was, by all means, desirable, some shrewder person than his neighbours was pitched upon to perform the part of a prophet. This person was wrapped in the warm smoking hide of a newly-slain stag or ox and laid at full length in the wildest recess of some lonely waterfall. The question was then put to him and the oracle was left in solitude to consider it. Here he lay for some hours with his cloak of knowledge around him and over his head, no doubt, to see the better into futurity; deafened by the incessant roaring of the torrent; every sense assailed; his body steaming; his fancy in a ferment; and whatever notion had found its way into his mind from so many sources of prophecy, it was firmly believed to have been communicated by invisible beings who were supposed to haunt such solitudes.

– Dwelly's *Scottish Gaelic Dictionary* (1911)

# I

In the Gaelic Garden of the Dead I am lying passionless, water-spent,
whose dream-traiked crystal, water-stolen, falls –
obdure, you rustic mirror of shades, whose high wall is breathing
grim, water-scryed intent.

With water cells shrunk about the waist I walk,
                                   paths of cinnamon at my feet,

where vultures fang bone on the sandalwood trail,
fang leaky meat from the old gang dule,
skulk the dusted dream-thief pile.

My shade is spiked with flowers
                 gently lifting in my shadow,
whose parched fire grew garden dreams, dire dule-trees,
row on row, sparkling in the mud.

Shriver-grief shrunk too late, in dream deteriorate:
the pause, my tears, the suffix,
parched hand-strewn, leaking.

Coaxing the woods,
saltire of fire
                gags the derangement mouth:

Coaxing wood from my swollen eyes –
crawling about their cinder pile,
wood densely compressed with unfelled tears
my lids now rust around stoppered drops
I pause to coax their harrow-juice –

                            Unkindled eyes!
                 Unkindled breath! Unkindled throat!
                     My lustral tongue, my lustral tear.

## II

I was young on hope and en-wildening expectation,
in the colour bitterness of this Gaelic garden.

Such star expulsion, canker-witted and rotten,
gave fumigation to souring dreams, furnishing the loss
of new rubbed leaves, ones stun-crushed by disbelief
into freshly perfumed poison.

Witless and stark they rustled; the darkling sedge
bloomed the last of its bud-punctured petals,
searing through tightness like nettle wands
brandished in whipping tips when the next season brightened.

What canticle of water-star root, hereditary dip-water,
flea-water chosen; that bright-hipped, blushed black
when the fires were scrying and I wept in the sod-dark
of vegetation weakened with flame.

The hedge-lip of stars and dereliction,
water that stains the grief of its own tremendous gestation;
nothing being taken without thoroughly knowing
the symptoms of its undertaking.

And simmered young, mummies thrum,
paste of sugar-fly, paste of polywater tree
and soldered to my eyes plaster-stars moult
flakes of preservation.

In youth I walked that fire-addled garden
the concubine of rusting trees, now filled with lumbering bees
and no-one to siphon off their sweetness,
while the wild glen raged with the last of the roses –

filaments of ashen compression
like the ashen faces each lyant morning,
ashen in the weak crease of dream,
compressed to the early ingredients of diamond.


### III


In the cave, the moon-holstered statue mouths:

'O stag, sole kiss with which the mute mouth burns!

O my sleep –

I saw you as a hologram
that came to kiss me
without touch
and turned back and forth
in a frenetic shift
and fixed there,

I awoke broken.'


### IV

Fang my water-throat!
My bone in the throat!

Where in the wind deceases
the ceaseless chattering trees...
You cannot tame the summer heat
that licks into your elbow crease,
that lashes wet kisses to the sticky brow,
that crawls down your back on sopping knees,

cannot hold the summer tame, in a hand of
shaken nettle-wands, nor curb its drowsy

guillotine, that keeps
all shadow cut.

Among roots of softly singeing wort-pearl,
love-slept charms of the underworld,
winter-slept in oils of peat,
your tug of hair,
your dirty ringlet:

in mow it sprigs the young green night,
in mow from deep golden bowels
trowelled from medieval bells,
swinging dule-thick rope.

## V

Angelic cultures grow between the rocks
planets of ash-hollow suffix:
what wary weight of dead sea fruit.

Tears of black diamond, sprays of golden dust,
the carnelian valley shuddering in lust
and the merbell-black rainbow oil, milky forelock dropped
and handled by the school of the moon.

These bramble dancers.
These mineral trumpets.

At long last licked my thumb in time to the dew.

## VI

In silence eater, in silence water
I come down to shade.

Whisper-tranced my panic belt,
whisper-tranced to consequence.
Where sweats the doe, aurora-spiked,
her panicked musculature,
shudders rustic at the wind's young touch,
schadowed in her pelt.

Mellifluate she pours, the honey hour
ourgilt, now lyant stands her wood.

The spriet trance backlights my brain,
comes woods, comes fighting –
lossless, your fall, tomb-strung, water-flayn,
ruby glanced she stands.
och, the dolour-schadow wind,
a running sore,
flows on rustit leaves and flowers
and my eyes, run dry,
keep changing colour.


## VII


My ancestors, conceived in woods,
brought night-shine onto other love,
when all our eyes were upon them, made
ribbon of debating soft wood from hard
in nuance love, in sedging heart
in all eradicate pulmonary blossom.


## VIII


Scorched with water, swollen with fire,
from burning lungs charred ash rises,
floats in tinder-slow dispersal,

17

turns in a brutal undertow of slow
unrealised dreams.

Fungus fingered the lyre-skinned schadow
blackened with the tip of hollow,
crumbling in the tower of silence,
rusting in the butcher's garden.

My silver finger-wood, lithe shadow-hood,
musked on silence, in milk-sprigged dark
where the stilled silhouette, recharges dreams
like a dying battery, like a bayonette,
squeezes them in the damp armpit, whispers
them into cascading hope.

I sing, they stream, I flee:


## VIV

I, water-scryed,
static the fear rises – floats wary-high:
>                         burning passionless harrow-juice,
>                         burning the anti-conjured corpse,
I sleep it off.

Fang sleep! Fattened for the trail: jail is the inscription I keep track of.

Lying at the feet of the thief-dream-school
against the wall, one shade-claw slowly raised
against the cave-garden mane,
how listlessly bewails, the sleep-flayn
>                     waterfall.

# PACE 2

## SUIT OF THE
## PLASTER CAST NERVOUS SYSTEM

SCOTSMAN DR HUNTER is considered the father of modern embalming techniques because he was one of the first to successfully inject chemicals into the arteries to preserve human bodies, then publishing his processes. Via the femoral artery he injected oil of turpentine, oil of lavender, oil of rosemary and vermilion. He permitted the chemicals to diffuse through the tissues for several hours and then removed all internal organs. The viscera were soaked in the same chemicals he had injected into the femoral artery, replaced in the body cavities and covered with camphor, resin, and dehydrating salts which were packed into the mouth, nose, ears and other openings. Finally the body was placed on a bed of plaster of paris to absorb the fluids.

# I

The sea is a wet fire in four grades of heat,
a salt ash field, salamandrine diminishment
of leached wood-ash slumbering, copse of falling plaster snow, syphoned
from death's vein, O Nile,
              finds your waters quitting, now

night has poured out lunar ash,
where this scrubland sticks like a tear-stiff eyelash, resistant
to your river's flesh

where, along your banks, among the reeds, you
can just perceive
escorticati down on their knees
vigorously rubbing their natron wounds – o Nile –
                      must I be one of these?

Whose waters broil in putrid stock; oil
of lavender, turpentine, vermilion, burnt
sugar paste and saliva western –
whose nilometer marks
the subtle quibble of temperature's persuasion –

Egyptian fawn-light greets them,
hand fed by a tiny speck of darkness,
stranded where the tide deceases and sits back,

              to watch the ravening.

# II

Vulturally speaking, I watched it spread itself, for all the world
like a strait jacket unpeeling in slow motion:
water that included the genesis of human expression.

21

Vulturally speaking, o intravenous cross that spikes,
spikes deep into the waterous tracts that lie
unprotected save for its bobbing, vicious presence,
drawing up nile-water tears for the mummified
stags that vulturally speaking, I wish to consume.

Vulturally speaking, I am ravaged
by the excess of my own seeking
whose salt water silts the drum,
o pinioned glass harmonium –
in loch water I drown and
– gripped – sleep fangs my mouth.


### III


O Nile,
I see you as a young boy,
waist high in water, urinating

your new-found gait, still heavy
with the risk of sleep, your catapult
of colour bitter stars, lazily welters at the hip,
your robs and waifs of crucifixion wood,
your Osiran bubbles quake in the heat, reeking
of solemn Egypt

that runs, dripping,
through your young cupped hands,
drinking galaxies of nectar, sucking flower pollens in the dark,
standing in the suckling milk
                              of your swelling shadow's counterpart.

Where you kneel, the grasses come, aching
for your silky feet –

they dance so hard it is
silence in the hour glass
shaken into wonderment.


# IV


Walk along your beach, who seethes,
in Tutankhamun's smile, who weeps
who nor by dreams was made to wash
in rough, indifferent seas.

What cross-bar have you helped?
What water divided you did not know about
as your Osiran bubbles float,
hand blown tears of grief stricken gods,
wicked on reeds of ash and honey,
litmus reeds of burning shadow,

as King David pants next to bright entrails, as the stag,
coral antlered, sings its death trials:

'On bended knee, I plait my will,
on blue, plump rushes, my coracle'


# V


O Nile,

you have hunted!

Some storms surrendered,
some – blinkered – ran wildly for the trees like the trees
themselves shedding bark, reverse chameleon, in swift succession –

Nine cured stags have rutted on my cardboard coffin:

you have hunted these!


## VI

Dimly, putrid putti speak, their pitted eyes
for hours glance down the stars, perceive
the fire so far as yet and sighing, evolve
mouldy toes and mossy cheeks:

the amber fountain growing colder.

Lonely fountain, in districts he keeps
his back to the fire alarm of heavenly gates,
remonstrates with park keepers and paper bag drunks
and drags the water across his tongue
as if licking roll up cigarette gum,
and watches the evening take.

Even fresh Nile-urine, poured through the mouths of petrified boys,
cannot keep him unguent, cannot
sift porous stone from storm –
fountain shade is all that seeps

movement onto pockmarked flesh;

those delicate stone-rolled genitals of monumental leaking angels, now
grown green and orange mottled.


## VII

In water woods and black-cured woods
we go walking. By moonlight the forest,
plaster-cast, is struck white and un-nerving. I have
run along my lover's bones and though not a
westerner yet, shuffle through their sugar dry leaves.

Come upon me! Come upon me in such a darkness!
Take me by my very eyes – secede!
Secede the now departing, granular dark, whose substance fades sheerly now,
in acquiescence to your burnished arrival.

Who staggers, shall be spoken.
Even though nine clots of fire pace low
and green in the thick of your brain, igniting
plumes of fiery sight, shall be spoken.

And great tracts of burning water that cross the palm,
back and forth in char-water paths
whose phosphorescence scars
the halo-clarted angels, smarting in the searing light,

> shall be spoken.

And sand punished back to the hour
where, loosed from glass, it once escaped
from time, o Nile –

> does day have courage as night slowly drains?

## VIII

As time gently files your diamond mirror – frightened –
shall be spoken.

Here: mark the deer blue-black in Nile-light,
here stand, hovering among the men
who continue frenetic self-preservation
rubbing sweet oils into their rigid veins.

Now all is calm in the firmament,
whose swollen waters course vermilion,
whose flinders rush at the great sob-moon
a torpid threshing – pale Egyptian barley tips moving

with the wind of time across the banishment,
shall be spoken.


## VIV

The tide-mark of the dream's secret is its own illusion.

   The visitation is moving.

Her death wish flickers, beached,
where Tutankhamun steeps –

Drunk on halo-water, a welt of angels rises
rash red on my vision to inform me of my mistake.

             And they sing, but it's more a kind of coagulation,

a rising note of perished firing –

a fire tone of back tense;
pearlescent cindery bead, an own voice for stoning angels

– for I am half mad with angels –
and would syphon halo-water from my own eyes
to desiccate their current sight

that now runs wild, turns to fissure, seeded long
by white grasses, parched
by flickering long white grasses…

and I am down on my knees,
             o Nile.

# PACE 3

## SURROIAL MORDANT SUIT

'The wounded deer leaps the highest'
– Emily Dickinson

# I

Berserker fawn, you tightened
the watermark of air,
                    gave glass cramp.


Dew beater of petroleum – a whole garthe trailed
in aerated fire bloom


a cross-pollination of blossom oil and orange foam whose star,
startling, rises
                    drugged fresh from puffballs, dust fungus from shaken down
poisoned tress –


deal your beaten gold leaf pack
lay out lagoons of rising lunar ash,
shuffle diamond crushed plunge-baths.


Gold-tongued fawn... tears glittering
whose mouth forms sweet bitterness,
whose storm-wrecked milk
assizes eyes of unguent, well-springs of bad fortune...


you never drank less than violet,
hoof pressed to expulsion, tears on heat in the sob-forest's wake,
tears on heat, clenched in the listing heart –


O golden fawn – your raving pirouette – I have met its darkness yet,
in young, cruel shadeless song of harp


whom air from shadow exfoliates
in a blizzard vial of storm-flung petals, spreading underwater
fawns, divers for the dead sea fruit.


O I have raised your ravening shadow, bitten
down on your silhouette.

## II

Ash covers his spectacles,
besmirches the deer
within his sight;
their coral-capped antlers run ragged
red and velveteen
and fixed in diamond light.

## III

Whose suspicion is fuelled by the ready turbulence of stars,
whose back-draught is the sultry moonlight,

Aye, she shy matador, sapling in the tall evening
bruised his velvets with an offering of blood,

Crystallised, in the fever-dreams of a shaken stag,
stumbling up to find his escape,

And there the arena stagnates, the kaleidoscope
arrests on its brittle rust.

## IV

Fawn flayed by diamond.
Night-hung, adamantine.

Propellor on the roof, cessation.

Drill bit over the pantomime
panting, o panting.

Whose breathlessness necessitates
hi-wire dancing.

Rewound quicksand

running late.

He stands in stripling tartan.
He stands in the while-whet current,
anticipating.

A bubbling need-fire of red coral amulet
the deer-spray, gone velvet,
stripped and hung from
shattered antlers.

On a salt-lick rubble
shore, whose deer,
now aquamarine, stall
in Northern coral.

Stand stock still
as if merbelled
with catastrophic secret.

Meal of hairskin
and guilt.

A salt lick god
smithereened upon the beach
aches to be lapped
back together again.

But wait, the tide takes
its own tongue out
and in
and out again
along with
fragments
of hands and feet.


# VII


Whose early progress was fire-dream,
a failed Brooklyn dance audition,
> failed by the city's ambitious water-bed,
> failed by the city's Indian-pestle, grinding for success,
> failed the length of his dumb-bejewelled skeleton.

New York:

a kaleidoscope of calcified sewage,
her scrapers pyres of unicorn bone,
flick-switch rainbows of drying blood,
stands like a stylite on her highest fruit-machine
blowing clouds of parti-coloured smoke.

So Christ-cast down, stands chain-smoking with a paper-cut tongue.

…was it in Queens a lookalike Nick taught
> mouth to mouth swearing?
Who eventually 'made blood brothers of them'?
Who, wrist slit by a lost shard of TV glass,
> shattered, circa the first moon landing, broke

amid the colour bitterness of consenting stars
among knights, whose persistence
is something to do with regret, yet know

he has swum with murrain-stained hands,
with ankles sawn off at the feet.

Nine of diamonds, o diamante teeth,
all the world's disappearing blood stains
reappearing at his feet,
in escapee guise of evaporate bleach
in a resurrection pie of broken meat.

Thissledown and how he came to appledom…
wandering concrete orchards, washing plots of rubbish,
scraping down diner-vinyl dinner-sets in cheap Brooklyn restaurants,
bursting through backdoors of downtown cathedrals,
sluicing liquidised stained glass, o chalices.

Flicks an American Spreit,
o wands, and it flares like an underwater faun
spitting through the back tense of rising street,
splitting hair from aerated water
whose chimes scintillate the arc
of dark notes headed water wide
for the churning Hudson river.

Burning confetti at his feet,
begged me not to wake him up,
o cowardice swords, windscreen wipers
or terror urine divining rods,
begged me not to wake him up

whose mind, covered in lichens,
all those crystallised first fruits
doused in diesel, the pillow stuffed and shaken,
took up a disposable sandwich board
advertising newly carved cherry stones

a sleep rivulet, polluted silk,
reappearing bloodstain at his guilt,
o kings,
that butterfly kiss of bleach – neat-sweet
takes his sin on the gum,
in late-night mastication

or single hair in the mouth,
of slender electric fence,
on carbonated water of all-night-light saliva
flower press of stilettos at my feet
bottled bonsais for the master

sleep a set of disposable teeth
figureheads writhing at still-bleeding feet,
knaves,
the ground littered, o, with dead chimney sweeps
the stakes – hired grief
on one side bubblegum, the other native chewing gum

yet he sucks buckfast on a small hand sponge
his card fast red, fast asleep,
whose rising cities, cherry-stoned, slump curtain-blind,
the new dawn grove fruit machine
begged me not to wake him up.

For three days after, the heart punched in –
dings to the sole temperament,
sight-lines of firemitts,
the anamorphic scaffolding
forces lights down – his eyes dropped, faltering

from whose palms, disappointed chrysalises form,
glittering spasms of car-light luxuriant
whose spangled middle gleams,
the long probe – trefoil-dark and gilt with gems –
a cluster-fuck of crucified fawns.

His perfume dispenser broken,
stretched in blocks, the whole garden an enticed lisping
chained by one ankle to a collapsing face
like a semi-automatic weapon dancing into wet incense
incised in barques of smoking peat.

## VIII

Then he bursts in flames of laughter,
burning light on bleeding snow –

of lovers in their scarlet circle,
of breath bent double in the nose.

His frosted whiskers strung with dying men;
with fire bit flame finds confetti in the trees.

His words die inwards like the nose,
his mind escapes incontinent.

A parapluie of stinging nettles,
A parapluie slung on the arm
To sting the rain with panther wings.

Cleans his ash hole arms.
The heart is appalled.

Leap into the star stable of madness,
god is movement, death is –

## VIV

Last night: I open the door
to a man chewing diamonds
with a roseate cicatrice – blood-shot mark
crossing his face –
a brilliant dawn of damage.

Where he stands in the flare-shot light
working his feed in leather and jet,
a shadow strikes him:

instant set of antlers.

It's only the yellow yew outside
and an old telesweving set
who conspire to make him less than human
yet it's true

that stagged he looks barbarous in the electric light,
transformed by stasis – bellicose –
the grand engineer of the rolling eye
thrown into the hands of a silhouette.

And it strikes me too, as I make to speak,
the dangers of frames that clasp the forms
of unrealised ones,
as I stand holding his unwavering gaze –
a strop for sharpening the razor blade.

# PACE 4

## SUIT OF THE ELECTROSTATIC RIVERBED

'I hae the saul o' a unicorn'
– William Soutar

# I

How listlessly, how listlessly,
the surging hour is given.

How flickerith the sizzlin' robin's nest
sequestered in faulty neon,
                bluid-blue the erroneous
crows digesteth myth of pelican –
a young, flashy, devouring carioun who binary *flares*
all or nothing, stabs
at light and dark.

How querulent the unicorn,
gently quivers in underwired neon,
                seized in ultra-pink and slot moon violet
his tender tresses fixed,
sits alone in chemical
his flaring tip of fissure volts, cranked
by the minute – jolts –

powdered flank and ankle bone: cracked plastic casing
tucked under him, sits alone with a lapful of charms,
waiting for the fuse to come

who comes confused, re-horned, re-shoed
in stapled gaffe tape, whose palpitant anti-poison sticks,
glow-in-the-dark needlework – expectancy waits,

O hovering horse, shone shoulder cold

            all night behaves,
as fossilised dead fire raves – a junket of wishing stones
themselves, young, dire and trapped
in the bright clasp of ageing promise,
cusps the shut blue river banked on jewel-fawns:

escorticati with flashing hand-guns,

the magic body, stalled in wet grass, stuns.


## II

    Stumbler among the tombs, chawed
to bits the electric tether, sudden pelt-flashing for the heather,

sad stiff little unions, piles of written-off symbolisms:

O jump-start horse, running high and dry on the mountain range:
        How slows the lonely tornado? How stills the rustit waterfall?

How your sweltering ego sits
on the fingertip of flashing prayer,
river-dizzy, now alights on the
two-tap flame of temperament:

        O a thousand Scottish churches burned not to have you come!


## III

On electro-static riverbed –
                your burnished throne – straps flung down,
currents strayed – fused in weird water expulsing colour:
in hue-rock, hope-lock broken down,
fissure jawing longer the dissent of flank
conjoined with tackle.

Electro-static elocution: on tongues were ye broken,
brass tack tongues and stool,
in leaking oils of corroding combustibles,
petroleum charms fastened
firm with guttural expectation.

Your exploitive pulsation – the long stare trained
on horizonhood.

Need flame, your trained chance, flickers at your hooves.
The coloured smoke of bad effect, redolent of epithet,
volting down the river's face

streams.

## IV

Your outlawed parts are courser, yellow,
steeping in the map of silence,
sweating out the pulse of poison:

> You have waited weeks for grief,
> You've consumed its fire-glyph,
> You have wiped its salty myth –

Icicle switchblade,
> fetlocked and forelocked on broken thermometer
> lisps in silk, redoubled lining,
> belted in water, belted whining,
> silence the watermark of air
> splicing an electric fence as you would split a hair.

> You swim the tuning fork of dark.

## V

Everywhere Christ's vulva, cultivating garden flowers,
who flocks, he sings: and strokes their heads with sparkling rings:

cultivations for certain books
forest of apple tree, holly and roses

salt lice unicorn, mer morte,
one delicate grey-blue with a shorter horn,
sickle shaped, like the sickly moon,
a yellow clay mound stuck with a rib,
a miniature creature grazing bonsai groves:

he lifts the glove and there they appear:
in flowers, moved by the wind.

And Adam's life shines
in hours shorn from unicorn bone
in hours blown through unicorn horn.

Scratched strange heads peer through the hedge;
jesters, the flowers jeer –

'Who taught *you* first to sing?
Your hard-rooted tongue swivelling?'

On crumbled teeth you came,
on crumbled teeth toward the flame,
crawled toward the mirror's reckoning,

unicorn with a coiffured tongue; worried and slightly ironical;
we never know what it is you are thinking.

Flagellant of glass,
your hornliest self come to graze
                              at the mirror's salt-rimmed edge,
                              at the mirror's cocktail spectacle,

choreograph of plastic calyx, diamante-quizzical:
your gaze a bouquet of dispersing
                              moths
     flashing on
and flashing off –

# VI

'Who goes there?'

– the broken twig, adamantine choir.

Night lifts its chin,
recallibrating, listening in.

> Barque of sawdust,
> Barque of silt-water,
> Barque of relentless, surging backwater:

Sculling fire-stained trauma
with oars of milk, of wood-churned mire,
on escalators of silver fire
icing-sugar rims your eyes;
belladonna, deadly nightshade.

Your face a grimoire of chemical reaction,
whose sob flinders rush
at the Big Bad Moon –

Lunar conquistador, moon-froth of river foam,
magnesia baubles your lucent loam,
the bitter taste lasts long on the gum.

# VII

I know your grief is a swimming chin
raised against the jewelled current,
in waters scintillant,
through rubies the colour of pigeon's blood,
cornflower blue and pinkish-orange sapphires,
liquid filled feathers and crystals of zircon
you circle, slow tears running, your own
residual, bitter colouring.

## VIII

Fire-flaught and trembling, fluent in flame,
whose trance-shackled gaze runs un-tame across fire-swept glass,
whose lucent stain runs a streak of rain across all your denuding selves,
pounding on fire-salted darks.

Fire-blubber, rainbow tamer, rainbow-blubber
your mordant tincture, hand-slaked by flame, ribboned, twists
and rises in ululating gorgeousness –

Your fall first wild rotten vegetable,
passes through
                    rootless animal,
                    soulful mineral,

peels out of your trenchant pelt,
sparkle-muddled element,

past skid-marks of the fire-shocked demons,
                    swims the diamonds,
                    oil-black waters,
                    flame soused pyres,
                    necro-rainbows,
                    watergaws of poisoned blood.

## VIV

Ungentle, you went under
and rose you up again
in the undertow whose crest you rode into –
anger – all animal signs cast asunder...

Beneath baited breath you rage:
agitated undertaker.

# PACE 5

## SUIT OF THE
## RUSTIT KALEIDOSCOPE

KALEIDOSCOPE 1817, LITERALLY 'observer of beautiful forms,' coined by its inventor, Scottish scientist David Brewster (1781-1868), from Greek kalos 'beautiful' + eidos 'shape' + scope, on model of telescope, etc. They sold by the thousands in the few years after their invention, but Brewster failed to secure a patent. Figurative meaning 'constantly changing pattern' is first attested 1819 in Lord Byron, whose publisher had sent him one of the toys.

# I

Lying on embroidered straw
he sleeps behind a waterfall:
bitten cheeked, dreams, on April-wood,
                  brent-tongued on thissle-down,
soft-rising seed bed, glade-punched his pelt and rising
– falling – sleep ribbed –

  his one hoof twitches –
busking blackness closes thissles,
          spreads in time with sunset,
that mould-furred cape, furls the thissle-witnesses
against the small fawn-sighs, against the luckless, sweetish simmer flies
that rise and glimmer-die.

# II

Storm arm of wood, darkening, the April-wood of Shepherd king pipes,
blows glistening baubles, glaring secrets with a haar-wind. O shelf of life
on your strip, blood bubbling between your lips:

he has leapt in the womb of his country, bucket bound
with slops.

Where young pan clops, cropping
                at the tight rose bud; little salty chrysallis,
chops the root of growing hope,
the awkward teeth,
champing at the pipe's thick bit;

sucking thissle pollens in the dark, standing in the suckling shade
of his swelling shadow's counterpart that now
                    runs wild, turns to fissure, seeded
long in the whitened grasses, parched long
in the flickering white grasses…

# III

Stone-oils swirl harder, milk of steel and aluminium foil
a treasury of unguents distils
in the space behind his eyes, refills.

You lisp with coping. You whistle-pitched hoping,
coddled sensation; the thissles glittering, hold conference at his feet.

One eye turning, half asleep, glowers into dream
and locks, rustic kaleidoscope, static-clicked –


# IV

     The sawdust in his hair,
       when he woke up, spinning silverleaf,

reads all meaning from the wind-moved trees
       and trains his shout to quiver.

Survived on robs and waifs,
the bejewelled jam of thieves
stones his vision higher into the stone-eyes
of carved ancestors, combed in fetlocks of shy-water, in blushing arts
      for water,
who locked their cocks with sleep and stroked them, softening,
into petrified relief –

Shoots of gold and wax melt. The arena runs around itself,
great thumbprint of eye, smudged along Orion's belt,
firmly pressed, chest to dust onto himself –

## V

Peered down the occultist telescope,
shifted the shattering gaze of centuries
with rusted kaleidoscopic irises;

blinked volcanic cataclysm with the mechanical
dynamism of plaster-cast anatomy skinned of secrecy
in salt-ash planets of dissected lunacy
in stars of erupted teeth –


## VI

Saw him sitting on a rock
                              with his mouth open,
devouring sunlight through his zero

And some say the moon –
a chemical apparition –

washes into being the heart soil:
moon seeded, moon pasted,
conjured not, only tasted.

About his head the tightening band
                    of stags that run around his brain,
                    well versed in the dictionary
                    of the moon.

# VII

Burns with a diamond trust,
the scape of salt-soaked rust.

Lids his flames, finds the boys watching
like deer, from saline soaked shadows,
from the salt soaked shadows that line the shore like grass:
an accomplice, limp footed, ignores them.

Sitting, leans in, scores,
breathing damp dust in, lining the wager in his lungs
with circumscribed hope.

What a watchdog.

Those bitter lozenges sculpted in heat
of a long island-changing day;
around the circumference of his nation –
precious stones.


# VIII

His diamond nib is broken,
broken in the diamond fog, clouded
with carnelian waters blooming
dark dust fields of gold that lie
languishing, reflected in

the ancient kohl that rims his clouded
eye, O Nile.

Reeking of solemn Egypt,
rise up o his sugar-cured hands,
furta sacra of diamond wood,

o sugar-cured stem of kaleidoscope
rise up, rubies the colour of pigeon's blood
liquid-fill with eagle feathers and crystals of zircon,
glowing red-rot blue, fluoresce ultramarine tears.

Mineral inclusions of wild cat eyes
wither-cold, bedecked stars gleaming
velveteen green, well emeraldine,
so hard mined from Egyptian stone
whose magnetic dreams seam blood-shot
tourmaline grown queasy
with a slight moon's
contaminated shimmering.

And dispersion is the origin of fire in gemstones
whose rutile feeling plumbs the dark as targum,
the sea-sung stone, as chrysolite whose hue
of undried ripe straw ignites the black-blueish
halo of bruise beneath a bulging onyx heart.

Fire opal and water opal grow lustrous-cold,
ash lagoons of lunar slake,
encrusted with flashing trails of dead sea fruit,
shadows of colour pounced in light,
ululating fire-bloom groomed in the stirrup oil
of dense compression.

Whose quiet tides keep lustre fire tight
locked up whose diamonds resilient
to the dusts of chrome, of skin,
of quartz and talc, resilient to
the sufferings of ruby-shot which blue-rots
its own colouring suffused
with other residual feeling...

# VIV

Went skating on the first mirror,
conveyed on motes of whistling dust.

               Pollen rose from thrashing robes,
whose poisoned hem gathered round
   anklets of raw-dusk bone,
   snow anklets –
   destruction of rain anklets,
suckling on the beauty carcass,
rose-luck rotting at his feet –

In winter, he prevaricates,
loosening the stakes
sucked the lens clean at your feet
sucked the clear marrow of hate

his antlered throne of prow-sin, falling
               whose glass colosseum ploughs behind him

Drowning,
takes breath in a new season
and plunged beneath again, drowning the welter of rainbow
rises, choking, re-callibrating
colour trystedness:

Dons emerald-lensed fighter glasses,
             bottle-ended spectacles:

         vignette figures in dust, fighting.
        tiny violent sawdust parlance,
       beleagured bleeding,
               strikes out
        on shattered glass...

# PACE 6

## SUIT OF THE FURTA SACRA
## OF ROBS AND WAIFS

'I SHALL BRING a stick to you that will keep you from harm in any brawl or battle… make sure you keep the stick safe, it will deliver you from all hardship and peril – it was once in the courts of Pharaoh.'

– Calum Ruadh, 'Fairy Song of Skye'

## I

O my broken stick of honey wood! My lightning
eucalyptus rod! Aye, petrified
my cherry rood! Ore crushed marker
of the listless pith of stars where wormwood
drowsing colloidal, sucks clean
gemstoned fire-marrow.

## II

O my witch-lit broom, cross-propped
for alighting – whose virulent roseate
wilts: flame wilted necklaces of hand-bunched
herbage, listless in the hand, about the neck
yet lucrative.

## III

Or my pole of infamy bled, whose anamorphic
expression smears like bruises across swift
likenesess; brought sudden to senses
by your sleek cylindrical mirroring
cross-hatched with curious mis-understanding.

## IV

My sugar-gless sword; brittle cutlass
of the wind, spun in stained colour,
comes to sun, droops melting,
comes to cold, invigorating, brandished
in the hours, slashes through the hummingbirds.

## V

Whose rogue toothpick of wild plum stone,
filed to dental point predatorial,
wild needlework upon the gum,
pricked to fetlock, the small chip-whip,
loosened all his bejewelled teeth.

## VI

My sea vehicle of scrimshaw rood
bursting blubbered water open, seeping
the oil – unguent of black maritime eye,
hangs from your cross-bar scaffolding
the long canvasses of the sea, painted by
storm-wind and dashed birdling matter, a banner
of manifold speed impressions and moving
water.

## VII

Or my shipwreck in a bottle!
The mute glass moils with the stoppered
cries of drowning men, destroys the sails
of sandalwood, the small paper shark's fin
in glassy waters gliding...

## VIII

Or my lucent horn, poised and sweating
harbouring an arboretum of poison
in night-tanged lucent dreaming, in
a colour-bitter distillation
of creamed off sweat, slowly churning.

## VIV

Plowtered in Egyptian mud,
o my battered old Nile bone,
water-quivered, river spliced,
tipped with the Osiran heron feather,
gold lingers on your lip, nilometer;
the watermark of vanished disbelief.

# PACE 7

## SUIT OF THE FAIRY CROIS TAIREADH

'IGNITING THE CROIS TAIREADH – nine men of 81 employed
to rub planks (roods or crosses) the function of these is to
create the right kind of fire to burn the sticks into an ash
ready for the underworld.'

– Martin Martin

# I

Incendiary, the fairy flag,
where fire spangs warp
the way of dreaming peat,
leaves red-baited mounds
of ash lagoon ciphering
encrypted zero.

And long-plunge the ash,
freed from colour-bitterness
to fetch in greyish clouds
a series of winds
within its plumes of dust.

# II

In thissle shaped fog
they prance, netted surroial –
mordantless, belching swathes
of parti-coloured ash, leaping
defenceless undertones, pronged
in kaleidoscopes of peat.

# III

Drops his eyelet,
feels it stud the ground,
encompassing a mis-en-scène,
a rotted vision of an old peep show
populated by half-burnt stags,
raw where the ash has not rubbed in,
dancing with their meaty tongues,
goring the night with doleful bellowing.

# IV

Stag crystal plumbs
his eye, back and forth,
pendulum, seeks his sight lines
trysts the diamond, o cruel dust
magnificent wrapped in a sack
of stripling velvets glued with
stag spool and honey stool
of the nightingale
and filled with the furta sacra
of robs and waifs.

# V

His propellor, sweating photograph, burning face,
criss-crossed with flag, pinned to his panting chest.

> Sugar-gless wings, o wings of jet,
> encouraging bludgeoned hope.

The cripple-cropped deer, munching galaxy
sleep in the pyre mounds of great deceased stars
in manacles of dust,
in manacles of steel,
his spectacles desist to seal:

no burning aviator repeals,
his dive-bomber pocket fills,
his razed sun-goggles of arena steam,
his photographic amulet steels itself.

## VI

Avian wound man,
your bird-brent wind of appetite now circulating, plumes
the necrotic dust of wills; showers us with the
leaves' wild guesswork; anti-conjuror of tornadoes
you walk to work

on paths of seed-vessel
and white-water bed straw
curdles the vetch-water in your sleep.

Who quivers, stills.

Choke-water glitters on the leaves,
he who stumbles, stuns,
the distant quiverer, pelted in swannis pen.


## VII

And who fell to his knees spattered with fire!

Left handed, red-rotted in clots of flame
a flaring deck flickering – nothing cuts
to the cochlea quite the same as burning petroleum;

I have heard the burr of clotted fire,
rise in a plumy air-plashed flock –

an incendiary flock of clotted angels
sugar-cured, bound in paper wrappings,
and rustling past the ear...

fire mitts in the coral, fanning –
whose ash-riffled spines collapse –
o long flames in the marrow of croft bones!

In air rimed nine with clouds of thissle-ash perspiring
resettling on the glove in a haughty clot of of bird
this misshapen carbon aerates as hawk,
shaking down cinderous feathers
grooming damp ashy down.

## VIII

How timely his nutrient slaughter,
where the tropic folds a little
wetter, the sinking tune of its evolution,
piped in whinny pips of birds

whose wild sweet wings in under
twenty four hours will seep their
tint into death's young gaze,
paint his lips with spectrum's brush
of fading war, of fading sex,
of fading flocks of moving colour

feathers dulled to blanche and till;
useless

       for the water-pen,
       for the arboreal,
       for the stilted quills still quivering
       for the tinted water, bloomed with foliage of the bright bees and
          the dark –

This is bloomed in blood.

## VIV

Nor by dreams, wind scalded, did he stramp
the depth of his reason
to disentangle branches of dirt-stone and gentle stone
in the cracked loop of angel voices.

                           The visitation is moving.

Nor by dreams did he gather the schadow
of plaster-cast statues whose sweat, in beds of natron,
lies gleaming.

And nor by dreams, in whose cupped hands licked
by coral-capped deer, did he tremblingly clasp the schadow of prayer
which musters ash in a ryatus wind while

on his knees he is scribing.

Nor by dreams did he whet the vision ash
of disintegrated wars on the tip
of his frightened tongue.

Once, at the other end of a gun, he brought a young stag down,
kend by effeir, and if it were he to slay him now as he here kneels,
he should take engranyt this offending.

Nine marks is he from death
and nine marks en-trembling.

Were he trammelled safe in lead, he should consider himself unfortunate
for it is only the deep-water wind of the river
that is his ploughing casket, or the matt and tread of the kirkyard floor
markit by the caerfull bees peteouse embraces with blumys
soon funded by his cair weid corse.

63

And nor by dreams fang his colour-bitterness!
Yet in the wilderness find him freshly fading –
such colouris of sight.

But though he is corsing water meat or flesh of turf,
nor by dreams is he dead:

she comes like a hawk, his punishment,
she comes like a hawk, like a nine of daemons, pushing for the glove

sees her bash air
on fire-fraught wings
                    and he is rad –

# PACE 8

## COLOUR BITTER SUIT

YOU START A crack in stained glass by spitting on it...

# I

O stained glass knight who stumbles

all night
through the sweltering wind, all the cardboard flames shaking
in his life's metabolism, his smile a butchered haunch of venison.

Diamond-blinkered his steed halts,
and in the broken glass bottles lining the roof of his mouth
the dream warp is colour-bitter, rising like heat off his sleep.

# II

Chain-mailed, copper eared, iron-lobed,
knitted cochlea, the shimmering pinna

and knights' tears
sent down the window pane in sluts of tears
and knights' tears
balancing on porous stone,
dogonis men,
waiting to sink doon.

Maliferous, questing tears, in questions of gloom
in the heart-sobbed dubloon of quarried lime:

bachilleris insisting on listening:
listless decipherment of silence
in shackles of shining armour
bachilleris of refreshed breast-plate:
copper flushed to rust, oxidised

brickish flare.

## III

Resting on the table of elements, his stone-rotted metal coat,
a petrified canal of meat-sloughed blood.

How rusts the waiting camomile in fields of starved canary
who lowers down his bright mine, the fast-panting bird.

Secrets of lime, secrets of wood-worm,
the mineral lantern stuck to the ceiling,
or gutted from light,
or carved in granite hope,
                    chiselled with geological luck.

## IV

Meat luck the hope swells,
gestating several centuries he smells on his arm,
joy, the lambent hound at his feet:
stone-suckler, stucco-breathed
shammy of leather-stunned dog,
mound of carved mail,
lint of copper sweet meat –
the grille of all kinds of hell beaten sweet,
beaten into tinfoil sheet
of snow and ridicule glinting in his flint-long sword,
buffed to pumice, a lava tongue, ashen with smoking –

he has heard it in his sleep,
has had it licked at his feet,
has washed it in the blizzard-heat
of tears, of railing tear-stone hails,
that fall to his knees,
                    in scabbardly suffering.

## V

If all metal magnetic,
all wood stone,
what difference his world
would become

what nature would
become his
alternate storms

and how would
the sunlight cease
to forget him
when in alliance
with

hard reflection.

But his halo
was only deer marrow
and he grew to hate
the necessary power
in his palms,
cross-charged with pain.

He felt full of snow,
marrow of farm animal
boneless void,
as the flakes originally decide
to resemble cold
only to dissolve.

Copperish his now new shadow
and his crumbling smile
a little longer.

He had thought fire
in pre-history
might warm him.

      Whose book is blinkered by snow fields of ash.
      Whose hands corrupt his face, when raised with coral sight holes,
      Whose halo light glows staunch mordantless.

## VI

Rocks; the rustit couplet o'erturns
the glowering hour bespoken.
The rivulet churns where
bastion to chain enslaves
his gold-panning hands

and smeared, Orion scores,
his bruised mouth tippled
with the scant remains of teeth
lowered to the river,
something of his reflection
assimilates in slaughter, drowns
in recent disbelief –

his wing-mirror, his fast arising bludgeon,
all conglomerate near the bottom
where thickly weeds clot a golden face.

## VII

Fat-palmed, pace-farmed in the
harrow flames of the long afternoon
all hatred walking out on water
left him disgraced, by nightfall,

by bank fall, kneeling, locked to mud:
your fear equips nothing; least
of all your stealth.


## VIII

O small whipping boy of a violent moon
did they thrash you soft with nettle tassels?
Did they welt your pangs of reason
with the hot seam of humiliation
did you stain that bank with treason, drive
it deep into the river's indifferent flesh?


## VIV

Your small oar, the needle hour,
working on the bottom lip,
your god-pout a luminette,
two-moon kept; schizophrenic locket,
the rustit rocket
chipped on kaleidoscopic secret
struggle-flamed – left gold prints on the prune-black turf –
on flakes of dried gold kohl
scribbling afterthought.

On your knees on the bank
now you gibber, aureole-stuffed,
genuflector.

# PACE 9

## SUIT OF THE DIAMOND SCRATCHED PANE

THE CURRENT Old High Church sits on possibly one of the oldest religious sites in Inverness. It is believed that St Columba preached here in 565AD and a wooden church was thereafter build on the site, then know as St Michael's Mound. Various structures followed and by 1746 the then stone built church had was reported to be in poor repair and was eventually rebuilt in the 1770s. Without question Inverness's darkest days fell after the Battle of Culloden, when it was said that blood flowed in the town's gutters. The Old High Church also saw its fair share of that bloodshed, 'the Kirk Session Records dated 25th August, 1746, refer to certain repairs which were required consequent on the use of the Church by the Government forces to house the prisoners captured at the battle of Culloden Moor. Those condemned to death were taken out and executed in the Churchyard. Two stones can be seen, near the west door, one with two curved hollows and the other with a V-shaped groove. They are nine paces apart and in direct line. It is thought that the prisoner, blindfolded, sat on the one, or stood or knelt behind it, while the musket of the executioner rested in the groove of the other.' The bodies of the executed Jacobites were then carried away by the poor folk of Inverness and thrown into a pit outside the church boundary or were disposed of in the river.

# I

In the muffled gong of blood,
                    acrobats of blood
never truly sleep, despite the fire resistance of their stock.


# II

Hard water seals around those on their knees –
even the river admits, he has sunk to drink-in visions.

And I am asleep outside my dreams,
where he who water-cast still stands,
in the slit-veined arm
                    of the torpid river.


# III

Gamble-washed in tumbling water, my hurt: spent, sluiced,
and made to mirror – who rinses in the river-mud
                    who draws the reed bed curtains closer
                    who sucks the root of rising colour,

nor by dreams have I withstood these,
nor by dreamer, anti-conjuring fallen blood –

                    twin dissected nightingales sing on my left wrist,
                              shaven,
                         damning it to red.

## IV

Who fine-tuned the thissles, wands of power,
in the night-paddocks of the grazing stags?
Who swims the tuning fork of dark?

Flame-soused with petroleum,
neutered with bald acts of forgetting.

## V

In forgetfulness, I have recalled the night.
In night the glowing merbell garden,
quarried chunks of
glowing supine white lumps growing
monumental in the darkness
hipped at twilight

                              withstanding ghost-flavoured wind.

## VI

Great regression of the river;
great regressive undertow
pulls his current into danger,
splitting seedbeds unto fissure
casting cracks of desiccation
sucks the waters deep into him.

## VII

I had heard water steals
its way through all such men
as a coursing deal.
They never really leave
the storm their hearts
made face upon,
they never really form
around much else.

Water-forms have spliced them,
brought them to their knees.

## VIII

I stand behind a frozen waterfall
comprised of universal blood.

A mirror and lens of suspended pain.
My reverse iteration: blood makes me the ghost
of my own slightly
moving form – frozen blood
dissuades my materialism.

If not a fool, I would find this amusing, I feel,
standing behind this sheath of glass.

My breath makes the first mark
on the flip-side of the waterfall: tremendous.

A pock mark in the ice-mane.

Whose warmth can dissolve the sanguine leap?
Can create a new river of melted blood?

I am terrified.
Waterfall tickling.

The red carpet at my feet descends to hell
and rises up again in a black rash
of glittering frozen road.

Beyond stellar, this altitude of pain.

My gash of breath is stifling.

I lick the salty streak
and taste the genesis
of my own dissolution.


## VIV

The tidemark of the dream's secret is its own illusion.
What wept, it seems, was poured in a glass of earlier dreams.

I downed it in one and kept the receipt.

*For Cairine MacGillivray*

# POSTSCRIPT

The title of this book is divided in two. *The Nine of Diamonds* is taken from an account of the notorious Duke of Cumberland, 'the butcher', who ordered that no quarter be given the Highlanders after the Battle of Culloden in 1746 and purportedly wrote the command on the back of a playing card – the nine of diamonds. As distant cousin to Prince Charles Edward Stuart, this hand – played whilst drinking brandy with his troops – can be seen as a kind of brutally familial after-dinner card game.

Structurally, the book is a deck of cards divided into nine suits, each of which has nine parts, to play the butcher back at his own game. The theme of nine is further explored through the nine pace execution of Jacobite Highlanders in Inverness Kirkyard after the Battle of Culloden; where prisoners were shot seated on a gravestone, nine paces apart from a mounted bayonet fired from a groove in the headstone opposite.

One of the most extraordinary Jacobite artefacts in the Special Collections at the National Library of Scotland is a moving eyewitness account by a wounded Captain Felix O'Neill, an Irish officer in attendance on Prince Charles Edward, written on a deck of playing cards mostly comprised of the suit of diamonds. This document does not include the crucial role the MacGillivrays played as part of the Clan Chattan, in being first to charge at the enemy Hanoverian line. The brutal consequences of the last battle to be fought on British soil have been well documented; the Highlands and Islands becoming a pockmarked landscape of rebel hide-outs in caves, dens and mountains. The form and function of this book is to play the butcher back; to confront the quarter which wasn't given in a performative reprise. The diamantine is symbolised through the waterfall that roars at the beginning and end of this Gaelic Garden of the Dead in which the characters as deer perform an extraordinary dance of persistent survival.

The second part of the title, *Surroial Mordantless*, is a concoction from an 1895 edition of the *Dictionary of Phrase and Fable* and refers to a section of stag antler – the 'surroyal' – and mordant (a dye fixative such as urine); in this case unsuccessful in fixing the running dye or blood of the allegorical stag as Highlander – and so mordant*less*. 'Royal is exchanged for 'roial' to reflect the displaced and disenchanted situation of Charles Edward Stuart; his demise as a scapegoat 'king' in France and to foreground a notion of rebel royalty – royalty demoted in the aftermath of battle. Ironically, this time for Bonnie Prince Charlie – his escape through the Scottish Highlands and Islands – brought him closer to the kind of Highland idealism and support his campaign had sought to promote.

So the deer run wild and they run through the visionary waters of the 'taghairm': the Highland numinous ritual of placing a man rolled in stag or ox hide within the innermost recesses of a waterfall to secure a vision for the clan. In a sudden leap, the imagery reveals a Surrealistic strain cross-germinated with the chance elements used to play the against the 'butcher', combined with the supernatural setting of the vision-seeker in the cave behind the waterfall. The book was researched at the Gabrielle Keiller Archive, Museum of Modern Art, Edinburgh, in the hope of finding some trace of a Scottish Surrealist movement. The scant material that mentions any imagery or theme relating to Scotland was gleaned for *The Nine of Diamonds: Surroial Mordantless*. I include poetic and visual resonances by André Breton, Marcel Duchamp, David Gascoyne, Mallarmé and Nijinsky to conjure a Gallo-Gaelic cultural landscape of mythic deer with 'coral capped antlers' (Breton), torpid gardens with 'thistle shaped fog' (Lamantia) and hyper-real waterfalls; '*Étant donnés* (Given: 1. The Waterfall, 2. The Illuminating Gas, French: *Étant donnés*: 1° la chute d'eau / 2° le gaz d'éclairage.)' (Duchamp). '*Surroial Mordantless*', then, whimsically echoes and displaces 'Surreal Mordantless' in an evocation and invocation of an alternative performance of Highland diaspora culture.

To initiate and navigate these themes and functions, the writing was aided and abetted by the Rider Waite tarot deck from which the figure of the fool is the most resolved manifestation, appearing vividly in Pace 3, the 'Surroial Mordant Suit'. This alternative deck was brought in to displace a more straightforward notion of gambling and to explore some of the more occult fascinations prevalent within Surrealist envisioning.

The rustit or rusty kaleidoscope also plays its part with many of the suits being summoned after using this 'prisoner's cinema' invented by Scotsman David Brewster and used by George Gordon, Lord Byron as a scrying device. The binary of this seeming conflict (and conflagration) of wills and positions: the myth of militaristic command transcribed onto a gambling card versus the more colourful but equally serious consultation of the tarot, necessarily reflects the dualistic friction seemingly obvious in the politics of the Battle of Culloden – of Lowlander and Highlander, of Catholic and Protestant, of Scottish and English. These opposites are too reductive and more than the sum of their parts and this type of complexity is mirrored in the book through a combination of seemingly disparate and therefore Surrealistic tendencies. Elements that bewilder and heighten the text are the use of the medieval Scots of Henryson and Dunbar alongside the practical and literary presence of motifs and phrases from the *Dictionary of Phrase and Fable*. The persistent undertow of magical imagery runs through diverse references to Scottish gemstones, early Glaswegian sugar embalming, the shackled unicorn and the MacLeod Fairy Flag; all interconnected within the visionary scope of the waterfall within the Gaelic Garden of the Dead. This waterfall, apart from being an obvious fall of tears, is tracked back to the River Ness which runs past the Inverness Kirkyard and which the Jacobite prisoners witnessed as the backdrop to their executions. Tallied with the age old myth of the Highlanders as a lost tribe of Israel and the early development of advanced mummification techniques developed in Scotland, the Ness is quick to flow into the Nile, where Scottish escorticati fill a riverscape of revivification and co-walking.

All of the book was influenced by direct experience – of the conviction of feeling the presence of Jacobite Highlanders unable to leave the kirkyard at Inverness, of the serious atmosphere in the cave at Elgol where Bonnie Prince Charlie took shelter during his last night on Skye – a cave which took five excursions to find, the startling presence of 'cat scratches' on the wall of the kirk within the MacGillivray enclave at Dunlichity made by claymore blades sharpened before the clansmen went to fight at Culloden; the MacGillivray 'Well of the Dead', the experience of being submerged within a waterfall at a Clearance Village on the Isle of Skye for the Gaelic film I made, *Aisling Sheòrais MhicDhòmhnaill: George MacDonald's Dream*, and in becoming a Gaelic speaker. The prismic quality of the diamond waterfall (one of compression released, of wept tears, of heavy drinking, of the Ness-Nile, of the scratched surfaces of vision) lends itself well to a Gaelic understanding of the spectrum which is more concerned with distance and saturation than the taxonomy of specific colour. In this Gaelic reading, the waterfall as a free-flow spectrum, unfixed and all-embracing becomes a condition, a state in which figures shape-shift into androgynous deer forms – creatures that stabilise and de-stabilise in urban and pastoral settings and are emblems of the leap. The leap might only be of faulty neon but it begins and ends with the waterfall, the visionary – even if necessarily failed. It is a leap that intrinsically Nijinsky – as faun – would understand, would attempt.

# NOTES

## PACE 1: SUIT OF THE GAELIC GARDEN OF THE DEAD

*Water-scryed:* divination with water.

*Cinnamon:* grows in a locked garden in the Song of Solomon, there was no trace of it in Egypt unless imported. 'A garden locked is my sister, my bride, a garden locked, a fountain sealed. Your channel is an orchard of pomegranates with all choice fruits, henna with nard, nard and saffron, calamus and cinnamon, with all trees of frankincense, myrrh and aloes, with all chief spices – a garden fountain, a well of living water, and flowing streams from Lebanon.' (SS. 4.12-15)

*Fang:* take, medieval Scots.

*Dule-trees:* hanging trees, medieval Scots.

*Shriver-grief:* confessional or written grief, Old English.

*Alexander Carmichael (Lismore) 'The Invocation of the Graces':* 'I bathe my palms/ in showers of wine/ in the lustral fire/ in the seven elements/ in the juice of the rasps/ in the milk of honey/ and I place the nine pure choice graces/ in thy fair fond face.'

*Colour bitterness:* to associate certain colours with disappointment or ill-feeling, *Dictionary of Phrase and Fable.*

*Rage:* take sexual pleasure, medieval Scots.

*Lyant:* grey, medieval Scots. (Traditionally grey is anathema to the Highlander.)

*I have a bone in my throat:* I cannot speak, *Dictionary of Phrase and Fable.*

*Mow:* dust.

*Dead sea fruit:* filled with beauty and promise but comes to nothing and is filled with disillusion and disappointment, *Dictionary of Phrase and Fable.*

*Merbell:* marble, medieval Scots.

*School of the Moon:* Highland school conducted at night in the art of cattle rustling.

*Schadow:* delusive appearance, reflection, medieval Scots.

*Mellifluate:* sweet (as honey).

*Ourgilt:* tinged with gold, medieval Scots.

*Spreit:* spirit, medieval Scots.

*Water-flayn:* water-skinned.

*Ruby glance:* gleam from a ruby, medieval Scots.

*Dolour:* sadness, medieval Scots.

*Rustit:* rusty, medieval Scots.

*Lyre:* skin, face, complexion, medieval Scots.

*Sleep-flayn:* skinned by sleep.


**PACE 2: SUIT OF THE PLASTER CAST NERVOUS SYSTEM**

*Allan Burns* was a Scottish anatomist (1781-1813) who first developed sugar-cured specimens (cured in marmalade) for the college street medical school in Glasgow.

The suit references the old myth suggesting that the Highlanders are descended from one of the lost tribes of Israel.

*The Nile* is interchangeable with the *River Ness* – see Suit 9.

*Nilometer:* cross found on the borders of the river Nile. A horizontal piece of wood fastened to an upright beam indicated the height of the water in flood.

It was said that *vulture claws* could extinguish fire in Renaissance palaces.

*Grip:* vulture, medieval Scots.

*Robs and waifs:* rob is from the Spanish for a sort of jam derived from the Arabic term for a piece of fruit. Waif originally signified goods a thief, when pursued, threw away to avoid detection, *Dictionary of Phrase and Fable.*

*'The Lord answered him not...nor by dreams.'* 1 Samuel 28: 6

*King David:* references the Scottish King David I who, according to medieval legend, saw the Holy Rood in the antlers of a white stag as he was hunting in the forests on the outskirts of Edinburgh during the twelfth century.

*Coral antlered:* taken from André Breton 'Postman Cheval'; '... holes through which stags with coral antlers can be seen in a glade / And naked women...'

*Putrid putti...* urine, poured through the mouths of petrified boys... alchemical reference in relation to the categorisation of heat and substance but here a short-changed alchemy – one which fails to procure an ultimate recipe but which, like Surrealistic contracts, instead defines a seemingly bizarre third element.

In ancient Egypt the word *westerner* meant someone who was dead, *Dictionary of Phrase and Fable.*

*Surroial mordantless:* the surroyal is a part of the stag's antlers; mordant is a fixative for dye, *Dictionary of Phrase and Fable* (see Postscript for spelling change).

*Berserker fawn:* the first part of a reference to 'L'après-midi d'un faune' by Mallarmé.

*Garthe:* an enclosed garden, medieval Scots.

*Puffball:* a fungus full of dust.

*Need-fire:* a superstitious and purposely cultivated wild-fire, *tein'-éigin*, to protect against murrain; the general term for diseases affecting cattle and sheep.

*'Ash covers his spectacles'* – references Breton and Duchamp in terms of the glimpse, and the occultist valley of dust bowl ash described in Fitzgerald's *Great Gatsby* in relation to the Ossianic 'desert' or waste ground which the Highlands was perceived to have become, during and post-Clearance.

*Red:* the colour of magic, *Dictionary of Phrase and Fable*, or advice, medieval Scots.

*'New York. Kaleidoscopic, grotesque... In the city of steel rhombuses ... Dazzling unrest in the blood of hermits.'* Leonid Feinberg, Yiddish Surrealist poet, *b.* 1897.

*'thissledown and how he came to appledom':* apparently the emergence of the Scottish thistle in America was through the commonplace use by pioneers of a pillow stuffed cheaply with thistledown and then shaken out to be filled with feathers. The thistle seed was dispersed on the wind.

*Murrain:* a mixture of myrrh and red wine offered on a sponge to crucifixion victims, *Dictionary of Phrase and Fable*.

*Resurrection pie:* a savoury dish of broken meat, *Dictionary of Phrase and Fable*.

*'Lovers in their scarlet circle'* references the diary of Vaslav Nijinsky who, when suffering a breakdown, hallucinated visions of lovers in the woods near his home and heard the voice of god. Nijinsky was famous for his extraordinary leap from standing and for his role as the faun in a ballet which he choreographed with a score from Claude Debussy's 'Prélude à l'après-midi d'un faune', both based on the poem by Stéphane Mallarmé.

*Telesweving:* television; sweving from medieval Scots for vision.


## PACE 4: SUIT OF THE ELECTROSTATIC RIVERBED

When Scotland is freed, the unicorn will be unchained.

*Carioun:* dead body, medieval Scots.

*'the magic body, stalled in wet grass, stuns'* in reference to Marcel Duchamp's last work: '*Étant donnés* (Given: 1. The Waterfall, 2. The Illuminating Gas, French: *Étant donnés*: 1° la chute d'eau / 2° le gaz d'éclairage.)' as declaration of the enlightened glimpse, the waterfall and connected to the assertion of the deer as female: 'the deer is the feminine element – the soul or anima the unicorn the masculine spiritus.'

'The horn is more powerful near the point than the middle... the best pieces are the whiter and soft pieces of marrow. The outward parts are courser and pale yellow-white.'

*Canst thou bid the unicorn with his band in the furrow?* Job 39:10.

*Icing-sugar rims his eyes:* 'belladonna, deadly nightshade' – trace ingredients found in Egyptian cocaine; traces of nicotine and cocaine trade with the americas or through trace elements of the substances in belladonna, herbage and mandrake, for example, that were known to the Egyptians.

Unicorns leap through the dish, as if in danger, a round dish of marble placed in a field.

It may well be that the unicorn horn does sometimes sweat like other solid bodies such as stone and glass, on which vapour and damp can 'freeze', that is – condense.

*Watergaw:* part of a broken shaft of a rainbow, Scots.

## PACE 5: SUIT OF THE RUSTIT KALEIDOSCOPE

*'L'après-midi d'un faune':* building on the presence of Nijinsky, this references Mallarmé's seminal poem as marking one of the beginnings of modern ballet and so the dance of the deer, evocative of French and Highland links in the 1700s and the association within Gaelic culture of Highlanders with herds of deer.

*April-wood:* the best kind of wood to use for making chanters in the Scottish folk tradition and referencing Robert Fergusson, 'On the Cold Month of April, 1771': 'Mute are the plains; the shepherd pipes no more'.

*Brent:* burnt, medieval Scots.

*Fog*: grass left in the fields during winter, medieval Scots.

*Red-rot:* sundew, *Dictionary of Phrase and Fable*.

*Stirrup oil:* a beating, *Dictionary of Phrase and Fable*.

*Light* is the source of all beauty in gemstones.

The Hebrew for the first named stone is ODEM, the root meaning of which is red.

*'Went skating on the first mirror':* loosely alludes to Sir Henry Raeburn's 1790 painting 'The Skating Minister'; Egyptian in its profile and seemingly antithetical in its depiction of civilised sport to the massacre of the Highlands which had happened only a few decades earlier.

*Emerald-lensed glasses:* Nero was said to have worn spectacles with emerald lenses to watch the gladiatorial fights. Pliny says the finest diamonds are green. Suetonius describes Nero as a bagpipe player: 'towards the end of his life he had publicly avowed that if he retained his power he would, at the games in celebration of his victory, give a performance on the water organ and the bagpipe.'

## PACE 6: SUIT OF THE FURTA SACRA OF ROBS AND WAIFS

Essentially, these nine poles constitute the oars for rowing the dead Highlanders across the River Ness as Nile.

*Furta sacra:* stolen relics, *Dictionary of Phrase and Fable.*

*Anamorphosis:* referencing the multiple Jacobite anamorphic constructions based on hiding the imagery of Bonnie Prince Charlie in everyday objects.

## PACE 7: SUIT OF THE FAIRY CROIS TAIREADH

'Always ready to fulfil their primary, military purpose, the men of a clan were traditionally called out by means of a the *crois taraidh* made from two pieces of burnt or burning wood roughly tied together with a rag soaked in blood and carried from glen to glen with surprising speed by relays of runners.'

*Zero:* indicative of the fool in the tarot.

*Thistle shaped fog:* taken from Philip Lamantia; 'shaping sand from thistle covered fog' in 'The Islands of Africa' (to Rimbaud).

During WWI MacLeod bomber pilots from the Isle of Skye would use photographic prints of their clan Fairy Flag as talismans against the enemy fighters.

*Swannis:* swan, medieval Scots.

*Stramp:* tread, medieval Scots.

*Ryatus:* dissolute, medieval Scots.

*Kend by effeir:* recognise by fine appearance, medieval Scots.

*'Markit by the caerfull bees peteouse embraces with blumys/ soon
funded by his cair weid corse.'* – Marked by the bees 'caerfull'
– showing signs of mourning – compassionate embraces with
flowers soon funded by his 'cair weid' – mourning – body.

*Colouris:* deceptions, medieval Scots.

*Rad:* afraid, medieval Scots.


## PACE 8: COLOUR BITTER SUIT

In the Gaelic, the spectrum is different from the one described
in English language. The saturation 'depth, or altered condi-
tion' corresponds directly to Gaelic definitions of colour as
outlined by writer John Murray. Here white is, for example,
'pale, lilac, bright and cold (fionn), pale, light, wan and fair
(ban) and clear, radiant and glistening (real). Fionn is mostly
found in the bright, sharp light of the north-west Highlands
and Skye. It can be confused with [...] Fionn the Fingalian
hero' from Ossian. The spectrum is not only observable but
experiential as a state or condition, closer to weather. This
subtle, alternative understanding of the condition of the
Highland landscape is coloured by weathering, distance and
stages of growth. 'There is a Gaelic saying,' notes Murray,
"the hillocks away from us are blue", which reflects the fact
that blue wavelengths travel further than red ones, which are
absorbed by dust in the atmosphere.'

*Bachilleris:* young knights, medieval Scots.

*Dogonis men:* worthless men, medieval Scots.

*Geological luck:* 'like a geologist I was about to turn up to the light some of the buried strata of the human world, with its fossil remains charred by passion and petrified by tears.' – George MacDonald, *Phantastes.*


## PACE 9: SUIT OF THE DIAMOND SCRATCHED PANE

Diamond scratching references the graffiti practice employed by Mary Queen of Scots and Burns (who had a diamond-nibbed pen) on panes of glass in the windows of houses they were visiting or imprisoned within. In this context, the frozen waterfall becomes a distinct pane of glass etched into by the feeling associated with the *taghairm.* The waterfall can be perceived as a frozen tear inscribed with the hieroglyphs of Highland consciousness as seen in the many men who hid in caves throughout the Duke of Cumberland's campaign of prosecution. The only quarter taken by those Highlanders – and not given – was most frequently in obscure cave networks, subterranean dens and in enclaves behind natural features such as waterfalls and, in the case of Bonnie Prince Charlie, hiding in a cave at Elgol, behind a stack of rock.

*Withstanding ghost-flavoured wind:* a nod to Ossian.

The burnt north wind creates an ash which, when compressed, is used to create diamond bullets. This artillery is capable of killing a man not through the mere insertion at speed of an alien object into his body but by decompressing on impact back into an ashen state which then, activated by the heat of the victim's innards, reasserts itself as a tempestuous wind whose dynamic force creates tornado-like conditions within the body of the attacked causing an explosion. The destroyed parts, however, are not merely dispersed but take on the attitude and likeness of the propellent – the wind currents – and so resemble a terrible dried but fleshy creature scalded and burnt in turn by the wind's conditions – a residual man of ash who configures and reconfigures on air driven currents never to fully resolve. This compressed ash simultaneously creates a diamond or diamonds: redolent of the diamond tipped dust of the north wind whose eyelashes are said to scratch the window pane of rural houses at night.

# ACKNOWLEDGEMENTS

With enormous gratitude to all those who have supported, enabled and encouraged my work:

A.R. Thompson, Luke Allan, Francis McGreechin, staff at the Gabrielle Keiller Collection at MOMA Edinburgh, Ronald Wilson at The Old Town Bookshop, Iain Sinclair, B. Catling, Geoff Cox, Andrew McDougall at the National Library of Scotland, Candis Nergaard, Damian James Le Bas and Delaine Le Bas, Tim Noble, Cairine MacGillivray, Steven Waling, Kate Tough, Juana Adcock, Henry Bell and Katy Hastie at Gutter Magazine, Janette Ayachi, J.L. Williams and Colin Herd at the Scottish Poetry Library, Kath NicLeoid, Meg Bateman, Murdo MacDonald and Hugh Cheape at Sabhal Mor Ostaig, Coinneach Lindsay, Ryan Van Winkle, Rob MacKenzie at *Magma*, Charlie Trier, Stafford Glover, James Young, Barbara Mercer, Christopher Willatt, Graeme Smith, Don Paterson, Tom Slingsby, John Davies, Anthony O'Donnell, Kristin O'Donnell, Nick Wong and Ian Smith at Creative Scotland, Rebecca Hind, Kate Gale and Mark E. Cull at Red Hen Press, Colin Waters, David Stavanger, Anne-Marie Te Whiu, Paul Daly, Andrew Spragg, Mark O. Pilkington, John Cavanagh, Donald Norrie, Nancy Campbell, Will Shutes and Jess Chandler at Test Centre, Toby Mottershead, Elaine Henry and Tarlochan Gata-Aura at Word Power Books, Alex Neilson, Craig Jenkins at Southside Books, Kate Davis, David Moore, Tai Shani and Roger K. Burton at the Horse Hospital, Lindy Usher and the ASLS.

MacGillivray is the Highland name of writer and artist Kirsten Norrie. Brought up internationally within a military context in Germany, Hong Kong, England and Northern Ireland, Norrie returned to Scotland after receiving a doctorate from the Ruskin School of Drawing and Fine Art, University of Oxford.

MacGillivray's first book, *The Last Wolf of Scotland*, published by Pighog/Red Hen (Brighton/Los Angeles) in 2013 (2nd edition, 2016), was written during a Kluge fellowship at the Library of Congress, Washington DC, on Shetland and Orkney and in the Highlands, and influenced by time spent in Arizona with Navajo and Hopi people supported by a travel award from the Slade School of Fine Art in 2003. Her second book, *The Nine of Diamonds: Surroial Mordantless* (Bloodaxe Books, 2016), was researched and written in Edinburgh and on the Isle of Skye whilst artist in residence at Sabhal Mor Ostaig, the Gaelic College, while making a Gaelic short film, *Aisling Sheòrais MhicDhòmhnaill: George MacDonald's Dream*.

MacGillivray has worked internationally as a performance artist solo, with the European collective *The Wolf in the Winter*, and with the *Parlour Collective* in Greenland, Germany, the Netherlands, Vietnam, the United States, Australia, the UK, Spain and Norway. Having recorded six albums, her music has appeared on film soundtracks for *Swandown* (Channel 4/Britdoc, 2012) and *By Our Selves* (2015), by British director Andrew Kötting and regularly on the BBC. She currently lives and works in Edinburgh.